THE AIR-BRIDGED HARBOR THAT **TWIN CITIES** FRAME.
"KEEP, ANCIENT LANDS, YOUR STORIED POMP!" CRIES SHE
WITH SILENT LIPS. **"GIVE ME** YOUR **TIRED,** YOUR **POOR,**
YOUR HUDDLED MASSES YEARNING TO BREATHE FREE,
THE WRETCHED REFUSE OF YOUR **TEEMING SHORE.**
SEND THESE, THE HOMELESS, TEMPEST-TOST **TO ME,**
I LIFT MY LAMP BESIDE THE GOLDEN DOOR!"

EMMA LAZARUS, 1883

"WHEN I DISCOVER A SUBJECT GOOD ENOUGH, I WILL HONOR THAT SUBJECT BY BUILDING THE TALLEST STATUE IN THE WORLD."

FRÉDÉRIC-AUGUSTE BARTHOLDI

LIBERTY

HOW AMERICA'S GRANDEST STATUE FOUN

FOR MY DAUGHTER, JENNIFER

DIAL BOOKS FOR YOUNG READERS *An imprint of Penguin Random House LLC, New York*

Copyright © 2019 by Robert Byrd. Photograph of Bartholdi on page 38: Musee Bartholdi, Colmar, reproduction © C. Kempf | Text contributions by Tracy Maurer

Penguin supports copyright. Copyright fuels creativity, encourages diverse voices, promotes free speech, and creates a vibrant culture. Thank you for buying an authorized edition of this book and for complying with copyright laws by not reproducing, scanning, or distributing any part of it in any form without permission. You are supporting writers and allowing Penguin to continue to publish books for every reader. | Visit us online at penguinrandomhouse.com

Library of Congress Cataloging-in-Publication Data | Names: Byrd, Robert, author. | Title: Liberty arrives! / Robert Byrd. | Description: New York, NY : Dial Books for Young Readers, [2019] | Audience: | Age 6-9 | Identifiers: LCCN 2018040742| ISBN 9780735230828 (hardcover) | ISBN 9780525554516 (epub) | ISBN 9780525554523 (kindle) | Subjects: LCSH: Statue of Liberty (New York, N.Y.)—Juvenile literature. | Classification: LCC F128.64.L6 B97 2019 | DDC 974.7/1—dc23 LC record available at https://lccn.loc.gov/2018040742

Printed in China | Design by Jason Henry | The artwork for this book was created using ink-line, watercolor, and colored inks on 140 lb. coldpress Arches watercolor paper | 10 9 8 7 6 5 4 3 2 1

ARRIVES!

HER HOME   *by* ROBERT BYRD

🏛 DIAL BOOKS FOR YOUNG READERS

INTRODUCTION

The Statue of Liberty rises tall and regal in New York Harbor. A powerful symbol of freedom, she has greeted millions of immigrants seeking a new life in America. Her solemn presence there for more than 130 years has been a constant reminder of the principles and promises in the Constitution of the United States. But the statue, Lady Liberty herself, had a long and uncertain trip to where she stands.

Born in France, the Statue of Liberty was to be the world's biggest birthday present to the United States for the nation's centennial celebration in 1876. Many French people admired America's ideas of freedom and liberty. They wanted to honor America's 100th birthday with something equally impressive—something grand, like America itself. The gift was to be like nothing else in the world, for a country like no other in the world. It was a big idea.

Big ideas are not small things to accomplish. The Statue of Liberty required creative thinking, planning, and lots of hard work. Many people helped, sometimes in unexpected ways. A sculptor designed it, and a bridge engineer figured out how to build something so huge. Countless craftsmen and workers constructed the statue and her base. A newspaper publisher spurred on a needed fund-raising campaign across the whole country. And the American people—immigrants, working folks, and even school children—came together to donate the money to pay for the mighty pedestal on which she stands.

This is the story of a most marvelous gift and the people who made it happen—and how Lady Liberty almost didn't come to stand in America at all.

THE BIG IDEA BEGINS

America had a big birthday coming up. In 1876, the country would turn 100! Years in advance, people were planning for the celebration. And not just Americans. In France, a wealthy judge named Édouard de Laboulaye dreamed of sending a gift from the French—a huge monument of some kind. He wanted it to symbolize liberty and mark the friendship between the two countries. Laboulaye had recently met a young sculptor who was becoming quite famous among the well-to-do Parisians. His name was Frédéric-Auguste Bartholdi. He would be perfect for this big project.

BARTHOLDI DREAMS BIG

Bartholdi loved everything big, even when he was small. He loved big buildings, big events, and big monuments, like the ones he saw when he was growing up in Paris. Bartholdi would explore the bustling city's wide boulevards and marvel at its towering sculptures. The 75-foot ancient Egyptian obelisk especially impressed him. Who wouldn't be impressed by 227 tons of towering red granite with elaborate carvings on its pedestal?

ABOVE: Bartholdi was not a good student. He often drew pictures of his teacher instead of paying attention in class.

As he grew up, he studied art, sculpture, and architecture with some of the best in Paris. When he was just ninteen, he convinced his hometown of Colmar to choose him—a teenager!—over an older local sculptor for an important project. The finished monument stood nearly 25 feet tall—too big to fit through the doors at

ABOVE: The ancient Egyptian obelisk was erected in the Champs Elysées in 1833, a year before Bartholdi was born and three years before he moved to Paris with his mother and brother.

the 1855 Paris Exposition. Instead, the bronze sculpture stood outside the entrance. Everyone noticed, of course. Bartholdi quickly grew famous.

Ancient Egypt sparkled in Bartholdi's imagination as he gained fame as an artist. In 1856, he jumped at the opportunity to visit the "Orient," as it was called back then. He stood before massive pyramids so tall they seemed to pierce the sky. The Great Sphinx towered above him. Bartholdi knew he could create big monuments like the Egyptians did, if he only had the chance. He was a man with a plan, about to meet Laboulaye and his plan.

FRÉDÉRIC-AUGUSTE BARTHOLDI

APRIL 2, 1834–
OCTOBER 4, 1904

Frédéric-Auguste Bartholdi's father died when he was two, and he adored his mother. Augusta (his middle name honored her) encouraged Frédéric's talents as an artist from an early age, and saw that he got the best art instruction in Paris.

ABOVE: Bartholdi traveled to Egypt with a group of French artists who admired the culture of the East. He photographed the great monuments of Egypt, fascinated by their colossal size. In these early days of photography, each photo took two minutes to shoot. No one could move the whole time. He also made more than 200 drawings. The Great Sphinx was partially covered in sand when Bartholdi saw it.

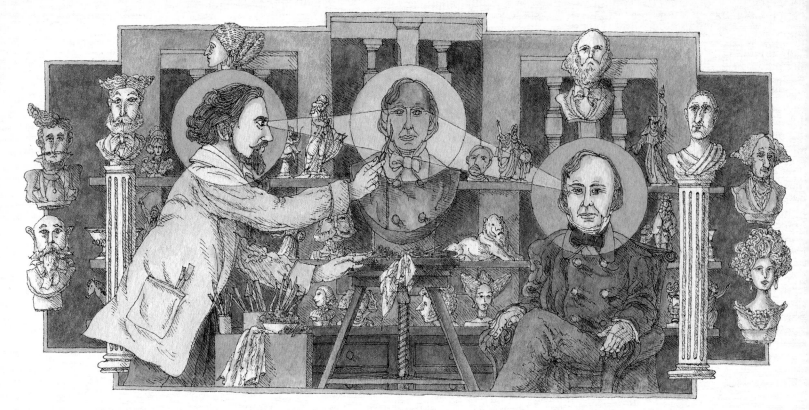

ABOVE: At this time, wealthy and influential people often hired artists to make paintings or statues of them. In 1865, Bartholdi was commissioned to sculpt Laboulaye, and they became friends. Bartholdi later wrote that this introduction would prove to be a turning point in his life.

HONORING AMERICA

Laboulaye had most likely chatted about America with Bartholdi back when Bartholdi had been hired to make a sculpture of him. He talked about the country all the time. America *this*. America *that*. He admired *everything* about the young nation—everything except its horrible system of slavery.

So, imagine Laboulaye's excitement when Abraham Lincoln and his Union Army won the Civil War and freed America's slaves in 1865. Such bold leadership! Such vision! Laboulaye had become a huge fan of Lincoln. Then, just five days after accepting General Lee's surrender to end the Civil War, the U.S. president was killed.

Now more than ever, Laboulaye wanted to honor the American democracy that Lincoln had secured. The judge held a fancy dinner for his friends that summer at his country estate. He invited Bartholdi, too. As they dined, the

Frenchmen listened as Laboulaye proposed creating a gift of a magnificent monument to the United States from France. Bartholdi grasped Laboulaye's idea right away. In his mind he began dreaming of something *big*!

ABOVE: Laboulaye cherished a letter signed by Lincoln, which he kept with his collection of American books and portraits of Thomas Jefferson and Benjamin Franklin. Lincoln's death deeply saddened Laboulaye and people in France, where he was greatly admired.

NOT SO FAST

The clouds of war in France stalled the grand project. In 1870, Germany and France went to war. Bartholdi set aside his art to fight for his country. Alas, France lost. Bartholdi was heartbroken. He threw himself back into his work.

Then, six years after that first dinner, Laboulaye invited him back. This time, the patron officially offered Bartholdi the monument job!

Thrilled, Bartholdi shared his big idea with Laboulaye: an enormous statue of the Roman goddess Liberty. He even had a name for her: *Lady Liberty Enlightening the World.*

Magnifique!

But would the Americans want a monument? Was there a place for it?

Laboulaye encouraged Bartholdi to travel to the United States to try to sell the Americans on the idea (although Laboulaye never once visited the country he admired so much). Bartholdi booked passage aboard the ship *Pereire* soon afterward. He arrived in New York Harbor at dawn on June 21, 1871, ready to meet America.

ÉDOUARD DE LABOULAYE

JANUARY 18, 1811–
MAY 25, 1883

Laboulaye was the first French scholar to teach American history at a university there, and he wrote several books about the new nation. He became the president of the French Anti-Slavery Society, and worked to help American slaves who were freed. He saw America's democracy as a model for France.

ABOVE: At a second dinner at Laboulaye's villa with politicians and thinkers and rich donors, everyone agreed that it was time to present the idea of the great gift to the Americans.

A HOME FOR THE LADY

ABOVE: The grand scenery of America enthralled Bartholdi. He captured the beautiful images in his paintings, such as Niagara Falls, shown above, and the Rocky Mountains, shown below, and the California redwoods, shown at far right.

Standing on deck as the ship entered New York Harbor, Bartholdi sketched the view. Sailing ships of all sizes leaned with the wind around him. At the turn toward Manhattan, he saw a small island in the entrance to the harbor. There! He knew this was the place for his statue. He envisioned Lady Liberty at the gateway to the New World, greeting new arrivals, a majestic reminder of America's democracy.

Fantastique!

More excited than ever, Bartholdi launched his American tour. He met many important people—famous poets, wealthy businessmen, senators, even Ulysses S. Grant, the president of the United States (who liked the idea of the statue). Bartholdi visited Philadelphia, where the Continental Congress had signed the Declaration of Independence. Planning was under way there for a grand Centennial Exposition in 1876 for America's 100th birthday. Bartholdi took note.

Everywhere he went, Bartholdi was utterly charming (of course!). Americans enjoyed chatting with the dapper Frenchman. They just weren't too keen on his statue idea. After the Civil War, they had roads to build, telegraph lines to fix, schools to reopen, businesses to run, and whole swaths of land in the West to settle and farm. Who had money for useless projects like this?

Some Americans felt it was risky business to accept such a large gift. Wouldn't France expect something major in return? Others argued the monument was impossible to build. And several critics thought the idea of a mythical woman holding a torch was too vague. Maybe a real

hero would be better. Still, Bartholdi remained hopeful.

TRAVELING COAST-TO-COAST

Bartholdi toured for six months. American cities were so much smaller and far less sophisticated, in his opinion, than Paris. But the country's immense size amazed him! Prairies rolled beyond the horizon. The Rocky Mountains jutted into the clouds. Giant sequoias guarded timeless forests. "Everything is big here—even the peas," he wrote home (the French preferred dainty peas).

He was certain his colossal statue was the right fit for this vast country.

Even without American promises for her home or help with funding, Bartholdi returned to his studio in France confident in the monument's potential success. Now was the time! He would create his masterpiece.

·Bedloe's Island· ✱ ·New York Harbor·

ABOVE: Bartholdi sketched Bedloe's Island from the ship, the *Pereire*. He liked that passengers on inbound ships would see Lady Liberty upon arriving to the United States. The island's unused fort was shaped like an eleven-point star. Wouldn't that make a beautiful frame for the pedestal? Bartholdi felt confident that President Grant would help convince the U.S. Army to give up the site for the statue's home. He could not imagine Lady Liberty anywhere else!

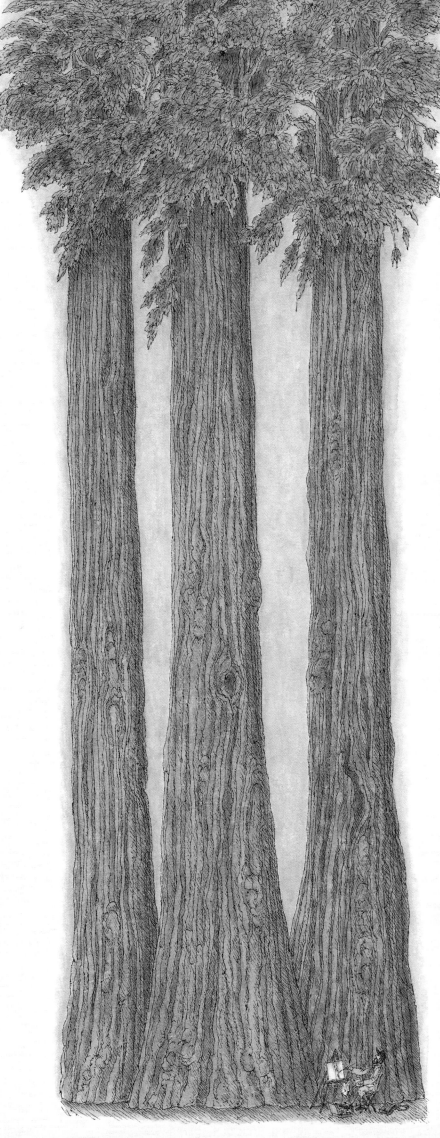

THE SCULPTOR SCULPTING

Back home in his Paris studio, Bartholdi focused on perfecting his sculpture of Lady Liberty. He'd proposed another massive female monument a few years back to honor Egypt's new Suez Canal. The deal fell through. Their loss! Bartholdi's new statue, Lady Liberty, would outshine any monument in the world.

He researched one of the Seven Wonders of the Ancient World called the *Colossus of Rhodes*, a mammoth statue of Helios, the Greek god of the sun. It stood about 108 feet tall. Bartholdi's Lady Liberty would stand a lot taller than that!

What would she look like? Bartholdi examined how writers and artists had portrayed the concept of liberty. The seal of France showed the Roman goddess of liberty, *Libertas*. She was

also on old coins and some American money. Inspiration struck. He sketched his Lady Liberty as the Roman goddess in a *stola*, an ancient Roman robe, with Roman sandals on her feet. He curled her hair in the trendy 1800s style to make her look modern, too.

MODEL AFTER MODEL

The sculptor earnestly began sculpting a series of small clay models, called *maquettes*. None of them stood taller than 48 inches. He tried new ideas on each one. Lady Liberty held a torch in her left hand in a few; she held it high in her right in others. Early figures had slightly turned bodies. Bartholdi settled on a forward pose.

The final version showed a broken chain at her feet, which Bartholdi had tried putting in her hand earlier, as a tribute to the end of slavery in the United States. Lady Liberty held a lighted torch in her raised right hand to symbolize enlightenment. In her left hand, she carried a tablet. Laboulaye suggested adding the date of America's independence—July 4, 1776—perfect for this centennial birthday present.

Bartholdi also put a crown on Lady Liberty's head with seven points shaped like the sun's rays, one for each of the continents. Windows in the crown would let light shine over the harbor. The torch might be used as a lighthouse. What a clever selling point! Bartholdi knew how practical the Americans could be; making the statue useful might help convince folks to pay for a pedestal for her to stand on, raising her high.

More than anything, Bartholdi dreamed his lovely little clay statue would become the world's tallest monument of its kind, the awesome colossus. It was hard for anyone else to imagine how a statue just four feet tall could do that.

Lady Liberty had some growing up to do.

ABOVE: Bartholdi dismissed claims that Lady Liberty was revised from his proposal for an Egyptian monument in 1867. The original figure, designed to be about as tall as Lady Liberty, wore a flowing gown and held a lighted torch to serve as a lighthouse. Coincidence?

ABOVE: Did Bartholdi use his mother as a model for Lady Liberty's face? He kept a portrait of her in his studio. They look similar. Then again, some people claimed that his brother inspired Liberty's face. Bartholdi never revealed his secret.

IT GROWS AND GROWS

Bartholdi unveiled his final sculpture of *Liberty Enlightening the World* at an elegant fund-raising dinner on November 6, 1875. The gala earned about $25,000—a good start. It would take ten times that much to pay for craftsmen, tools, and raw material. He left the money problem to Laboulaye, for the moment. He had a statue to make.

BUILDING UP

To build a structure almost fourteen stories tall, Bartholdi needed space, and a lot of it. His studio would never do! He moved his operations into a large metal workshop in Paris.

Next, he set up a "pointing" system to enlarge his small statue. The process worked in steps, doubling and then quadrupling her size. Each time, his workers built a wooden frame strung with plumb lines (strings with weighted ends) to make straight lines. They drew a grid on the frame, like graph paper. Workers made thousands of marks, called points, on the first statue. They multiplied the measurements from the points on the smaller figure to calculate the shape of the larger sculpture using the grid.

Because of its great size Bartholdi chose lightweight copper for his final work. He would need about 300 copper sheets, each just 3/32" thick—the height of two stacked pennies. Each sheet would be hammered into a wooden mold using an ancient process called *repoussé* (meaning "to push back"). Each mold held a reverse imprint of one part of Lady Liberty. So, where the statue's elbows bent out, the wooden mold curved in.

Bam! Bam! Bam! When the hammered copper sheet was popped from the mold and turned over, it held the exact shape of the statue. Rivets would stitch the sheets together like a quilt to form the final sculpture.

Bartholdi watched the s-l-o-w progress every day. He soon gave up the plan to send the whole statue for America's centennial. But maybe they could build one piece of the statue in time.

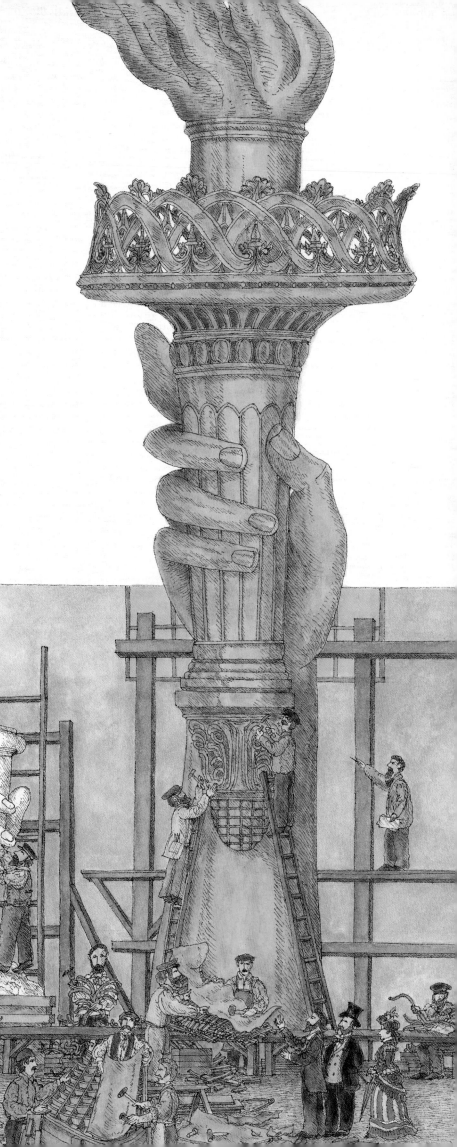

TAKING LIBERTY ON THE ROAD

THE PHILADELPHIA CENTENNIAL EXPOSITION, 1876

The Paris workers set to finishing the statue's right arm and torch by May. Meanwhile, Laboulaye organized the Franco-American Union to raise money in France for the project. He proposed that France would pay for the statue and America would pay for its pedestal. Exhibitions would surely convince folks in both countries to open their wallets.

The statue's arm section finally arrived in Philadelphia—in August, missing the July Fourth celebration. The delay only built up excitement. Crowds paid to walk inside the enormous arm and climb the steps to the torch platform. Still, the exhibit closed in November with dismal earnings. A similar showing in New York fared about as well. But the arm and torch remained in Madison Square Garden for five years. The American Committee of the Statue of Liberty was formed in late 1876 to lead the pedestal fundraising. Perhaps now the donations would flow in.

ABOVE: Visitors climbed winding stairs to reach the crown for a view from the windows.

THE PARIS EXHIBITION, 1878

Fund-raising in France started out better than in America. Then interest dwindled—until the Paris Universal Exhibition ignited public enthusiasm again. The event opened in 1878 with the great head of Lady Liberty on display. She was a star attraction! Earnings now totaled about $125,000—half of what they needed. Bartholdi jumped in. He made and sold small replicas. There were lotteries, benefit concerts and balls, and newspaper advertise-

ments. Even schoolchildren donated to the campaign. By July 1880, they'd reached the goal!

Bartholdi returned to the workshop, determined to finish Lady Liberty now that they had money. However, he had one (large) glitch. He had not figured out how to safely hold up her 32-ton copper shell. The artist needed an engineer... but who could handle a project this big?

EIFFEL'S IRON SKELETON

Bartholdi had planned to fill Lady Liberty with boxes of sand to hold up her shell. Most big statues were built that way—even the *Colossus of Rhodes*. But no other statue matched Lady Liberty's size. Bartholdi turned to France's most innovative engineer, Alexandre-Gustave Eiffel, to find the best solution.

Eiffel was already famous for his iron railroad bridges (his tower in Paris came later). His designs used connected iron beams, strengthened by smaller horizontal and diagonal beams. He adapted his technique to hold up Lady Liberty.

Her iron "spine" was the main tower, or pylon. It used four 15-inch-wide vertical beams that ran from four corners up 96 feet. Her supporting "ribs" were hundreds of smaller crisscrossed beams. Eiffel designed a separate frame that connected her upraised arm at her shoulder.

Attaching the copper was also a challenge. High winds could cause the structure to sway. What's more, iron rusts when it touches copper. Eiffel devised a brilliant system of metal loops set on the copper sheets. Small iron bars slipped through these "saddles" to ride the weather, separated from the copper by special padding. The iron bars linked back to the ribs and the main pylon. *Voilà!*

FAR ABOVE PARIS

By 1884, Lady Liberty was complete. She towered 151 feet over the thousands of awestruck Parisians below.

Sadly, Laboulaye died before then. Bartholdi carried on with their plan, ready to ship her to America.

But Lady Liberty still had no pedestal to stand on there.

ABOVE: Bartholdi treated important wealthy patrons to fine dinners, seated in Lady Liberty's gigantic knee. Moonlight flickered through the statue's rivet holes like stage strobes shining on the guests. Strange yet marvelous—it was a setting unlike any restaurant in Paris (or anywhere!).

ABOVE: During construction, Bartholdi proudly gave tours inside the statue. People entered the heel of her right foot (shoe size 879) and climbed stairs up her shin to her knee. Eventually, visitors could climb many more steps to reach her crown.

THE LADY SAILS

Meanwhile, the American Committee had been struggling to raise funds for Lady Liberty's pedestal. Theater galas, sporting events, benefit dinners—they brought in only a small amount of money. It was surprising anything got done at all. Comprised of wealthy businessmen, the committee members often delayed on decisions or quarreled with one another.

In 1882, the committee managed to hire architect Richard Morris Hunt, famous for his fancy mansions. It took over two years for the committee to agree on the pedestal design.

Hunt's pedestal plan called for a huge concrete foundation with walls 20 feet thick and 65 feet high. It would be the world's largest mass of poured concrete. That was just the foundation! An 89-foot pedestal for Lady Liberty would stand on top of it.

NO MONEY, NO PEDESTAL

In April 1883, the American Committee held a small groundbreaking ceremony on Bedloe's Island. Workers began digging a hole twenty feet deep for the foundation. They found bomb-proof shelters beneath the old fort that needed to be broken apart and removed. What a job! It meant more delays and more costs—soon the fund was drained. Work stopped in March 1885.

What would happen now?

Other cities, including Philadelphia, Boston, Cleveland, and San Francisco, volunteered to host the statue instead. Each claimed it was ready to raise the necessary money. Not one could guarantee it.

BELOW: Despite the bleak outlook, Bartholdi would not give up his dream. He ordered his workers to take apart the great figure they'd just built. They marked the copper sheets and iron pieces and packed them into 214 labeled crates for shipping by train to the port of Rouen. There they were loaded onto the French warship *Isère* for the trip to New York.

ABOVE: Thousands of people lined the shore to welcome the *Isère* and her cargo. Their cheers blended with boat whistles and horns, a joyful noise that wafted across the entire harbor. The French ship docked at Bedloe's Island and the crew made ready to unload Lady Liberty's crates. They had plenty of time—the pedestal was not finished.

Bartholdi could only imagine Lady Liberty on Bedloe's Island. He took the greatest risk of his life and arranged her shipment there, though he had no guarantee of funding.

Lady Liberty's crates filled the hold of the *Isère* when the vessel sailed from France on June 1, 1885. Some crates weighed 150 pounds, others topped four tons. The ship was built to handle heavy cargo even in the Atlantic's fierce storms. Still, the American Committee grew worried when the ship missed its expected arrival. Maybe it had sunk!

By the time the *Isère* finally sailed into New York Harbor on June 18 (to Bartholdi's considerable relief!), the city welcomed Lady Liberty with great fanfare. The pedestal fund, however, was still short.

ABOVE: Hunt's first pedestal designs were too lavish for the American Committee. He revised his drawings and shortened the height. Instead of granite blocks, he would use concrete covered in granite panels.

WHO CAN SAVE HER?

Newspapers carried rousing articles about the arrival of the *Isère* and the Statue of Liberty stacked in crates. Some reporters and other critics wondered if she should have come at all. The pedestal fund had less than $3,000. The U.S. Treasury rejected the American Committee's pleas for funding. In New York, Governor Grover Cleveland vetoed spending $50,000 on Bartholdi's big dream. One group of millionaires in New Jersey carefully considered the issue. After debating for hours, they decided to donate $20. Twenty dollars, not twenty *thousand* dollars.

The American Committee needed a whopping $100,000 to finish the pedestal; it seemed like an impossible amount. Philanthropy, the idea of giving generously to a worthy cause, just didn't happen then as it does now. Except for feeling good about themselves, the wealthy had no incentives to donate. People with only a little extra money to spare worried about keeping their savings for unexpected expenses. No one seemed willing to give.

JOSEPH PULITZER

APRIL 10, 1847–
OCTOBER 29, 1911

Joseph Pulitzer left Hungary at age seventeen, and he served in the Union Army during the Civil War. He bought his first newspaper company in St. Louis, Missouri. He later bought the *New York World*, reviving the failing newspaper. He was known for publishing articles that exposed corruption and stories that were written in a sensational way. Today, the Pulitzer Prize, a top award for writers and composers, is named for him.

ABOVE: An army of newsboys sold newspapers to passersby in the city streets every morning and afternoon. In New York alone, about ten thousand newsboys, mostly orphans and immigrants, hawked papers. They bought newspapers from the publisher, usually 100 papers for 50 cents, and sold them for a penny each. With no returns on unsold papers, competition was fierce—and loud!

THE GREAT RESCUE CAMPAIGN BEGINS

There was one important man in New York City who was disgusted with the greedy millionaires. And his opinion mattered. His name was Joseph Pulitzer, the newspaper publisher. Every day, thousands of New Yorkers read his newspaper, the *World*. In those days there were no radios, televisions, or computers. People found out what was happening from the newspaper.

Pulitzer had come from Hungary in 1864, leaving behind his family's wealth to make a name for himself. Pulitzer understood what Liberty meant to immigrants, soldiers, and working people. He didn't have patience for the rich elite who seemed to have forgotten the core values of the United States. To be honest, he didn't have patience for much. So, no one was surprised when Pulitzer began writing scathing editorials that mocked the wealthy tightwads for not supporting the pedestal. Word by word, he used his pen and his publishing power to try to save Lady Liberty.

THE POWER OF THE PRESS

"Read all about it!" called the newsies from street corners as they battled for readers. Joseph Pulitzer's paper the *World* was very popular. He knew that sensational stories, scandals, and conflicts sold the most papers. In the *World* Building in lower Manhattan, Joseph Pulitzer's office was on the top floor under a dome, while the editors and newsmen wrote stories on upper floors. In the basement, huge presses could print 48,000 eight-page papers per hour. Newspapers took sides on the sizzling controversies of the day, including the Statue of Liberty. Their impact on public opinion was huge, because newspapers were the only sources of information.

People usually had a choice in their city of two to five newspapers with morning and afternoon editions. Neighborhoods where people spoke little English might have a newspaper printed in their native language, too. From these highly competitive dailies, usually sold with just a few pages, folks learned about local and world events, politics, social affairs, and exposés (the nastier, the better). They were intrigued by the Statue of Liberty's story.

SUPPORTING THE PEDESTAL

Pulitzer had seen Lady Liberty's colossal head at the Paris Universal Exposition when he'd visited the city on his honeymoon in 1878. He used the *World* to remind readers of the pedestal

BELOW: People wanted to know the latest news back in the 1800s, too. In the days before everyone carried a cell phone to find out what was happening, people read their newspapers in the morning and in the evening.

The World

issue, running political cartoons that made fun of the stingy wealthy. He put the Statue of Liberty on the paper's masthead for emphasis.

Everyone knew where he stood. Not all agreed with him. *Harper's New Monthly Magazine* suggested the French should have given both the statue and the pedestal instead of just half of a gift. Other editorials from outside of New York City thought the statue wasn't really a gift for the entire country but only for the city—and that's who should pay for it. Some wondered if the monument was all that important anyway.

Pulitzer kept writing his editorials, leading the fund-raising effort now instead of Bartholdi or the American Committee. People must have liked what he said. They kept buying his newspaper—and its popularity kept growing. But donations were not.

All the while, Lady Liberty waited in crates on Bedloe's Island.

BELOW: Newspapers printed more than articles. Political cartoons were popular, too. These graphic images tried to sway public opinion. People who couldn't read or speak English could understand the visual messages as well as anyone else. Pulitzer used the cartoons to remind readers about the Statue of Liberty. Both cartoons below portray the statue as an actual lady, not the symbol she is.

ABOVE: Before the Linotype machine was invented in 1884, typesetters arranged each letter by hand using a composing stick (top of page). The Linotype machine above changed everything. Newspapers could publish more pages faster than ever. Linotypists used a special 90-key machine, similar to a typewriter, to set each line of type (*line-o-type*). Publishers and printers used this complex machine for almost 100 years.

Here the statue looks disapproving and disappointed as she reads in the newspaper that the pedestal is still not finished.

The statue is shown as an old lady who has aged during the many years she has waited for the pedestal to be completed.

PULITZER'S PROMISE

Joseph Pulitzer flat out rejected the idea of failure. He always had. So, knowing that America might fail at building the pedestal for Lady Liberty frustrated him—a lot. The lack of funds made him more ornery than usual by the spring of 1885. That's when he picked up his pen again and made a new plea. He asked his *World* readers to show the rich New Yorkers a thing or two about generosity and national pride. On March 16, 1885, he wrote a piece called, "What Shall Be Done with the Great Bartholdi Pedestal." He gave the answer:

Let us not wait for the millionaires to give this money. It is not the gift from the millionaires of France to the millionaires of America, but a gift of the whole people of France to the whole people of America. . . . Give something, however little. Let us hear from the people.

✧ ✧ ✧

Pulitzer made a promise unlike any before. The *World* would print the name of each person who sent money to the pedestal campaign and show the amount of his or her donation. It didn't matter how much people gave. A few pennies, or a few thousand dollars, every donor's name would be listed in the paper! How thrilling! And how clever of Pulitzer—he'd sell even more newspapers as people would look for their names.

The bold fund-raising idea was also risky. Just as Bartholdi had taken the risk to send Lady Liberty to America before the pedestal was built, Pulitzer was putting his reputation on the line. What if only a few people sent money? What if the campaign failed—and tarnished Pulitzer's glowing record of success and influence?

BELOW: Bartholdi returned to his studio in France to work on other projects while he waited to hear about the pedestal. He did what he could to help. For example, he published a booklet with the story of Lady Liberty that was sold as a fund-raiser. For a donation of $1, the *World* offered a 6-inch replica of the statue, and for $5 donors got a 12-inch statue.

PENNIES FOR THE PEDESTAL

Word spread across America about the *World*'s pedestal campaign. Donations soon poured into the New York office from as far as California, Texas, and Florida. Each day, Pulitzer printed in the *World* the names of everyone who had made a donation, no matter how small the amount.

Children especially loved seeing their names in the newspaper. They sent pennies (lots of pennies!), nickels, and dimes. They sent their candy money. They sent their allowance money. A few children mailed donations more than once, just to see their names in the *World* again.

To boost his plan, Pulitzer set up a system of "drummers"—fund-raisers who were paid to drum up donations from assigned districts in New York City. The drummers kept twenty percent of what they collected. Nothing like this had been tried before. Drummers asked everyone they met for a donation and promised to have their names printed in the *World*. Who gave without hesitation? Most often people born elsewhere with not much to give except gratitude for a new start in America. Both Pulitzer and Bartholdi hoped that would be enough.

ABOVE: Pulitzer published the list of donor names under a cartoon showing Uncle Sam holding out his hat in front of the Statue of Liberty. The caption read, "The *World*'s Bartholdi Pedestal Fund."

"Philip and Eliza Bender, 50 cents each; children—Anna, 25 cents; Frannie, 25 cents; Leonard, 10 cents; Alice, 10 cents; Ralph, 10 cents; Carri, 10 cents; Miss Nancy, 25 cents." —Philip Bender, Jersey City, NJ

"I enclose $1 as my subscription to the Bartholdi Statue Fund. I wanted to send more but my papa said $1 was enough from a little boy five years old."   —yours respectfully, Willie H.

"We children, brother and sister, send the sum of 10 cents for the benefit of the Pedestal Fund for the Statue of Liberty." —Nellie H. and Frankie O. Farnam

"I am a little girl nine years old and would like to do something for the Statue fund. I will send you a pair of my pet game bantams if you will sell them and give the money to the statue." —Florence de Forest

ABOVE: A kindergarten class in rural Iowa sent $1.35 to the fund.

THE PEOPLE SAVE THE DAY

The donation tally in the *World* grew and grew! Pulitzer shared the children's own words in featured stories to nudge adults into giving more. Along with contributions from children, money came from shopkeepers, doctors, bankers, soldiers, and sailors. The mayor of Buffalo, New York, donated his $230 annual salary. One of the most famous donations came from Emma Lazarus, a well-known poet in New York. She wrote "The New Colossus" for one of the pedestal's fund-raisers in 1883. Years later, her words would grace the pedestal and give the statue a special meaning for immigrants.

Together, children and adults heard Pulitzer's call for help. America's first "crowdfunding" campaign worked! Just as the Internet connects us today, the *World* newspaper brought people together then to contribute to Lady Liberty's cause.

On August 11, 1885, five months after the statue arrived in boxes on the ship from France, the *World* announced that about 121,000 everyday Americans had donated over $102,000. Most donations were less than $1 each. "The people have done their work well," declared the *World*.

The fund held enough money now to resume building the pedestal. With an imposing base to stand on, Bartholdi's great colossus would soon rise high above the harbor just as he had imagined.

BELOW: The pedestal was a grand structure in itself. Workers attached polished granite slabs to the huge concrete base, the biggest building in the United States at that time. The pedestal soared upward, eventually standing 89 feet above its foundation on top of the island's old star-shaped Fort Wood. On April 22, 1886, the last pedestal piece was laid. Masons tossed silver coins into the wet mortar to celebrate.

EMMA LAZURUS

JULY 22, 1849–
NOVEMBER 19, 1887

Emma Lazarus was one of America's first successful Jewish American authors. The hardships of Jews immigrating from Russia inspired her to write the sonnet "The New Colossus." After Emma died, her powerful words were engraved on a bronze plaque and placed on Lady Liberty's pedestal in 1903.

ABOVE: Once the pedestal was completed, metalworkers began constructing the statue's iron skeleton on top of it.

ABOVE: The thin copper sections, or the "skin," were lifted up on heavy ropes by a steam-powered crane. The pieces were maneuvered into their correct positions and fitted in place on the iron frame. Workers stood or sat on the iron crossbars and hammered the rivets that held the statue together. Some men sat on swing-like seats that hung dangerously suspended from the girders above.

THE FINAL WORK BEGINS

BEDLOE'S ISLAND, 1886

Bedloe's Island buzzed with activity once more. A small army of men, most of them immigrants, took up their tools. Workers had begun unpacking Lady Liberty from her crates (finally!). Metalworkers first had to erect Liberty's gigantic iron skeleton, and then fit in place the copper sections of the "skin," or surface. A doorway in Lady Liberty's right foot allowed workers to climb inside to stitch the copper shell to Eiffel's iron grid—rivet by rivet.

Assembly was slow at first. Some crate numbers had worn off. Other parts had the wrong numbers. Several sections had bent in storage. Coppersmiths had to figure out where the pieces went and then reshape them to fit. She would not be finished by July Fourth, as Bartholdi had hoped.

THE GIANT PUZZLE

The statue became one big puzzle that took six long months to solve. Finally, the work was done.

On October 28, crowds filled the city streets for a grand parade to officially welcome the Statue of Liberty. Bartholdi had sailed from France for the big day. The parade then headed out onto the water, carrying Bartholdi to Bedloe's Island to unveil his masterpiece.

Bartholdi climbed the steps to the crown, and peered through a window high above the harbor. Twenty-one years had passed since he and his friend Laboulaye had first talked about creating a 100th birthday present for America. The gift was very late, of course, but now it truly honored the people of France and America. All of the planning, fund-raising, and worry was worth this moment.

Bartholdi was excited for the unveiling ceremony, maybe a bit too excited. He pulled the drop-cord earlier than scheduled. *Oops!* The French flag covering her face fell away....

ABOVE: Despite rain and fog, more than a million people in New York honored Bartholdi in a grand parade. Afterward, they flocked to the downtown waterfront to watch the ceremony attended by the president, Grover Cleveland, and other dignitaries.

AND THERE SHE WAS

On her granite-clad pedestal stood Bartholdi's beautifully big idea, holding her lamp high: Lady Liberty Enlightening the World—one of the greatest gifts to America that almost never happened.

Magnifique!

MEASURING THE STATUE

When the statue *Liberty Enlightening the World* was inaugurated in 1886, it was the tallest man-made structure in the world. It is still one of the world's tallest statues.

Length of index finger:
7 FEET, 11 INCHES

Length of torch:
21 FEET

Length of hand:
16 FEET

Longest ray in crown:
11 FEET

Length of right arm:
42 FEET

Number of windows in crown:
25

Width of mouth:
3 FEET

Length of nose:
4 FEET, 6 INCHES

Length of head:
17 FEET, 3 INCHES

Length of tablet:
23 FEET, 7 INCHES

Width of tablet:
13 FEET, 7 INCHES

Shoe size:
879

OTHER MEASUREMENTS

Height of statue: 151 FEET

Height of pedestal: 89 FEET

Height of concrete foundation: 65 FEET

Total height: 305 FEET

Number of steps in statue from main lobby to crown platform: 377

Weight of iron skeleton: 125 TONS

Weight of the copper skin: 100 TONS

Total weight of statue: 225 TONS
(450,000 POUNDS)

TIMELINE

1865	Édouard de Laboulaye's dinner party where the idea for the statue is born.
1871	Frédéric-Auguste Bartholdi visits the United States and sees Bedloe's Island.
1875	The Franco-American Union is formed to raise money for the statue.
1875	The fabrication of the statue begins in Paris.
1876	Liberty's torch arm is displayed at the Philadelphia Centennial Exposition.
1876	The American Committee for the Statue of Liberty is formed.
1877	Bedloe's Island is named as the site for the statue.
1878	Liberty's head is displayed in France at the Paris Exhibition.
1879–1881	Alexandre-Gustave Eiffel begins the statue's internal skeleton.
1882	Richard Morris Hunt begins to design the pedestal.
1883	Joseph Pulitzer begins his first fund-raising campaign in the *World* newspaper.
1883	Emma Lazarus writes "The New Colossus."
1883	Édouard Laboulaye dies.
1884	The statue is completed in Paris.
1884	France officially gives the statue to the American people on July 4.

1885	The statue is taken down and shipped to America on the *Isère*.
1885	Joseph Pulitzer collects $102,000 for the pedestal.
1886	The pedestal is completed.
1886	Assembly of the statue begins.
1886	*Liberty Enlightening the World* is dedicated on October 28.
1924	The Statue of Liberty becomes a national monument.
1956	Bedloe's Island is renamed Liberty Island.
1965	Ellis Island becomes part of the Statue of Liberty National Monument.

MORE ON THE STORY OF THE STATUE

ABOVE: Frédéric Bartholdi posed for photographs—a lot. He took every opportunity to promote his work, especially his masterpiece. Here is Bartholdi imitating her pose with upraised arm.

OTHER BARTHOLDI WORKS

Frédéric-Auguste Bartholdi is best known as the sculptor of the Statue of Liberty, but you can see other works by him in the United States. Bartholdi designed and built a lovely fountain for the Centennial Exhibition—at least something of his was finished for America's birthday celebration! Later, the fountain was moved. It now stands in Bartholdi Park in Washington, DC. His other work in America includes a memorial to the Frenchman Marquis de Lafayette, who fought for America in the Revolutionary War, in Union Square Park in New York City.

A NEW NAME: LIBERTY ISLAND

The name Bedloe's Island, where the Statue of Liberty stands, was officially changed to Liberty Island in 1956. Nearby Ellis Island opened in 1892 as an immigration station. Immigrants fleeing oppression and poverty, or seeking freedom or a better life in America, sailed past Bedloe's Island on their way to Ellis Island, their first stop in America. Before they were permitted to enter the United States they had to pass through the main building there (below). Together Liberty Island and Ellis Island are now called the Statue of Liberty National Monument. Over four million people visit the Statue of Liberty every year.

SYMBOLS: WHAT DO THEY MEAN?

The Statue of Liberty is a symbol of liberty and freedom. There are other symbols on the statue. The book she carries is inscribed with the date the Declaration of Independence was signed, July 4, 1776, in Roman numerals. The seven points of her crown symbolize the seven seas, the seven continents, and the rays of the sun. The broken chain at her feet represents the defeat of slavery. The torch she carries symbolizes enlightenment—having a belief based on reason, education, logical thinking, lighting the way to freedom, and the spread of liberty.

ULYSSES S. GRANT

APRIL 27, 1822–
JULY 23, 1885

RICHARD MORRIS HUNT

OCTOBER 31, 1827–
JULY 31, 1895

Ulysses S. Grant led the Union Army during the Civil War and served two terms as president of the United States from 1869–1877. Bartholdi asked him to use his connections as a former general with the Department of the Army to assure that Bedloe's Island with its army fort would be designated as the site for the statue. Perhaps Bartholdi and President Grant talked about painting when they met. The president was a fine watercolor painter.

Richard Morris Hunt, the architect who designed the pedestal, worked for two years with Bartholdi on its design. He was very well known as a designer of mansions and elaborate homes for very wealthy people. But he also designed many other kinds of buildings, including early skyscrapers and grand public buildings (the facade and the Great Hall of the Metropolitan Museum, for example). He received $1,000 for his work on the pedestal, which he donated to the American Committee to fund the statue.

GUSTAVE EIFFEL

DECEMBER 5, 1832–
DECEMBER 27, 1923

ABOVE: The statue as she appears today.

Gustave Eiffel, a French engineer, first gained fame for his railroad bridges in the mid 1800s. Later, he worked with one of his employees, Maurice Koechlin, to create the Eiffel Tower—the first landmark "skyscraper" of its kind—for the World's Fair in Paris in 1889. The tower's ironwork is similar to the structural design for the inside of Lady Liberty.

FROM COPPER-COLORED TO GREEN

The Statue of Liberty looks blue-green today. She wasn't always that color. Her original copper shell glistened brown-orange, as lovely as a new penny. What happened? Oxygen, salt water, and heat reacted with the copper over time to form a layer or patina called copper oxide. This process is called oxidation. This blue-green verdigris shield protects the copper from further exposure. It took about twenty years for Lady Liberty to change color.

AUTHOR'S NOTE

Everyone knows the Statue of Liberty. She is as familiar to us as the sun and the moon. I only knew her from pictures—I never visited her until I started to work on this book. The most amazing thing about her is the most obvious. She is monumental, rising majestically out of the New York Harbor. What new could I say about her? I knew she came from France, but I was unaware of the dedication of a few enlightened people and their admiration for the ideals of American freedom that inspired them. The efforts that went into her construction with the labor of hundreds of workers and the perseverance of Auguste Bartholdi were astonishing.

I was happily surprised to find Liberty's whole journey was photographed, with many pictures on a huge scale, so critical for my reference and work. I could not have done my artwork without them. Bartholdi also understood the importance of photography as a promotional device. He hired photographers to document the statue's construction, and these pictures raised money and awareness in history's first major marketing campaign. Liberty's likeness was well known long before her celebrated unveiling.

I would have enjoyed seeing her standing in a Parisian street completely assembled before being taken apart and shipped to America. I still find it hard to believe she is made of copper sections only one-eighth of an inch thick. I have tried to tell her story as accurately as possible, and to give readers a sense of her long and difficult venture, and of the times and places she lived in. —R.B.

BIBLIOGRAPHY

FOR ADULTS

Bartholdi, Frédéric-Auguste. *Liberty Enlightening the World*. New York: Root & Tinker, c 1884.

Berenson, Edward. *The Statue of Liberty: A Transatlantic Story*. New Haven, CT: Yale University Press: 2012. Accessed online.

Blanchett, Christian; Dard, Bertrand. *Statue of Liberty (The First Hundred Years)*. New York, NY: American Heritage, 1985.

Khan, Yasmin Sabina. *Enlightening the World: The Creation of the Statue of Liberty*. Ithaca, NY: Cornell University Press, 2010. Accessed online.

Mitchell, Elizabeth. *Liberty's Torch: The Great Adventure to Build the Statue of Liberty*. New York: Atlantic Monthly Press: 2014.

Moreno, Barry. *The Statue of Liberty Encyclopedia*. New York: New Line Books, 2005.

Sutherland, Cara. *The Statue of Liberty*. Museum of the City of New York, Barnes and Noble, 2013. Accessed online.

CHILDREN'S BOOKS

Behrens, Janice. *What Is the Statue of Liberty?* New York: Children's Press, 2009.

Curlee, Lynn. *Liberty*. New York: Atheneum Books, 2000.

Kent, Deborah. *The Statue of Liberty*. New York: Children's Press, 2012.

Landau, Elaine. *The Statue of Liberty*. New York: Children's Press, 2008.

Malam, John. *You Wouldn't Want to Be a Worker on the Statue of Liberty!* New York: Franklin Watts, 2009.

Rappaport, Doreen. *Lady Liberty: A Biography*. Cambridge: Candlewick, 2008.

Shapiro, Mary. *How They Built the Statue of Liberty*. New York: Random House, 1985.

Silate, Jennifer. *The Statue of Liberty*. New York: Rosen, 2006.

Xavier, Niz. *The Story of the Statue of Liberty*. Mankato, MN: Capstone, 2006.

ONLINE SOURCES

NATIONAL PARK SERVICE
https://www.nps.gov/stli/index.htm

https://www.nps.gov/parkhistory/online_books/hh/11/hh11g.htm

CITY OF COLMAR
https://www.tourisme-colmar.com/en/visit/presentation/history/famous-people-from-colmar/176-auguste-bartholdi-father-of-the-statue-of-liberty

http://www.musee-bartholdi.fr/actualites/bartholdi-portrait-intime-du-sculpteur-lexposition

OTHER SITES
http://www.wonders-of-the-world.net/Statue-of-Liberty/Edouard-de-Laboulaye.php

https://www.newspapers.com/newspage/81851903/

https://sites.google.com/a/umich.edu/from-tablet-to-tablet/final-projects/the-invention-of-the-linotype-machine-jienne-alhaideri-13

http://www.linotypefilm.com/

http://www.pulitzer.org/page/biography-joseph-pulitzer

THE NEW COLOSSUS

NOT LIKE THE **BRAZEN GIANT** OF **GREEK FAME,**
WITH CONQUERING LIMBS ASTRIDE FROM **LAND TO LAND;**
HERE AT OUR SEA-WASHED, **SUNSET GATES** SHALL STAND
A **MIGHTY WOMAN** WITH A **TORCH,** WHOSE FLAME
IS THE **IMPRISONED LIGHTNING,** AND **HER NAME**
MOTHER OF EXILES. FROM HER **BEACON-HAND**
GLOWS **WORLD-WIDE WELCOME;** HER MILD EYES COMMAND